CHOCOLATE
BAKING

D0771891

CHOCOLATE
BAKING

LINDA COLLISTER
Photography by
Patrice de Villiers

RAINCOAST BOOKS

Vancouver

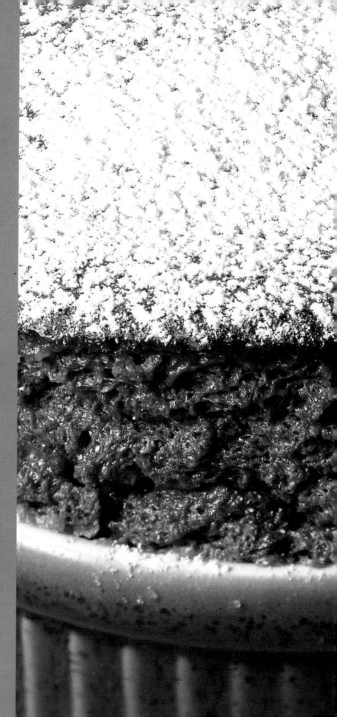

For Emily

Notes: Ovens should be preheated to the specified temperature – if using a fan-assisted oven, adjust time and temperature according to the manufacturer's instructions.

First Published in Canada in 1998 by
Raincoast Books
8680 Cambie Street
Vancover, BC
V6P 6M9
(604) 323 7100
www. raincoast. com.

First Published in Great Britain in 1997
by Ryland Peters & Small

Text © Linda Collister 1997
Design and photographs © Ryland Peters & Small 1996

Printed and bound in China by Toppan Printing Co.

ISBN 1 55192 203 7

Canadian CIP data is available from the publisher

CONTENTS

baking with
chocolate

Eating chocolate is **pure joy**, cooking with it a delight, even smelling it is bewitching, but buying it shakes my faith in human nature.

The best chocolate is wonderful, but most is not worth buying and most people buy terrible stuff. Good quality bittersweet chocolate will taste **smooth** not greasy, **bitter** not raw, **intense** not oversweet, with a **long finish,** not an excessively sweet aftertaste.

But how do you know good quality? Price is not a reliable guide—in fact supermarkets' **own brands** are usually excellent and are a good bargain when buying in bulk for cooking.

The quality and taste of chocolate is determined by the quantity and quality of the **cocoa solids**—the dry solids plus the added cocoa butter—used in its production. The quantity of solids, at least, is indicated on the package. **American bittersweet** chocolate or European **dark cooking chocolate** such as Lindt is best for baking. Bittersweet has around 35 percent cocoa solids, whereas Lindt—which is widely available in good supermarkets and specialty shops—has up to 55 percent. Couverture chocolate produces a very glossy surface, and is used by professional bakers.

The raw material for chocolate is the cocoa bean, found in the large yellow-green fruits of the *Theobroma cacao* tree which grows only within 20 degrees north or south of the equator. Each tree yields enough beans to make around 5 lb. of chocolate each year.

The best chocolate is made from a **blend of beans**—each type has its own individual character and color, ranging from pale coffee through to dark mahogany brown.

Store chocolate well away from other foods in an airtight container in a **cool, dry place,** because it can easily be tainted by other flavors. Avoid storing chocolate below 55°F, or in the fridge, as beads of moisture will form when you bring it to room temperature.

Don't store in a hot kitchen (85°F or above) or it will develop a white bloom as the cocoa butter comes to the surface. The bloom does not affect its taste however—it can still used for cooking. Chocolate begins melting at 85°F (that's why it melts in the mouth) and burns at 228°F. Melt it **slowly and gradually** as it easily becomes overheated and scorched, and turns into an unusable solid mass. Chop it into evenly sized pieces so it melts at the same rate. Place in a shallow, heatproof bowl set over a pan of steaming hot, not boiling, water. The water must not touch the base of the bowl, and no drop of water or steam should touch the chocolate or it will seize up. Stir **frequently**, and remove from the heat as soon as it melts.

almond
chocolate kugelhopf

2⅔ cups white bread flour

½ teaspoon sea salt

¾ cake compressed yeast

5 tablespoons sugar

¾ cup plus 1 tablespoon
skim milk, tepid

3 eggs, beaten

2½ oz. bittersweet chocolate

7 tablespoons sweet butter

½ cup slivered or flaked almonds

Nut Coating:

1¾ tablespoons sweet butter

½ cup slivered or flaked almonds

confectioners' sugar, for dusting

one 9-inch kugelhopf mold

Makes 1 large cake

*To use easy-blend dried yeast,
mix 1 package with 1 cup of the
flour. Mix in the sugar and milk and
let rise for 30 minutes. Make a well
in the remaining flour, add the
salt, add the yeast liquid and eggs
and proceed with the recipe.*

To make the nut coating, soften the butter and spread thickly inside the kugelhopf mold, then press the almonds all around. Chill while preparing the dough.

To make the dough, mix the flour and salt in a large mixing bowl, then make a well in the center.

Crumble the yeast into a small bowl, then cream to a smooth liquid with the sugar and milk. Pour into the well, and work in enough flour to make a thick batter.

Cover with a damp cloth, and leave at normal room temperature for 30 minutes. The batter should look bubbly.

Add the eggs to the yeast liquid, stir until combined, then gradually beat in the flour to make a soft and very sticky dough. Beat the dough in the bowl with your hand or with the dough hook in an electric mixer for about 5 minutes or until it becomes firmer, smooth, very elastic, and shiny.

Chop the chocolate and soften the butter. Add to the bowl, together with the almonds, and work in until thoroughly incorporated. When evenly mixed, carefully spoon the soft dough into the prepared mold (it should be half full).

Cover the mold with a damp cloth and let rise at cool to normal room temperature until the dough has almost doubled in size and has risen to about 1 inch below the rim of the mold—about 1 hour.

Bake in a preheated oven at 400°F for 45 minutes or until the cake is golden brown and a skewer inserted midway between the outer edge and inner tube comes out clean. Let cool for

1 minute, then carefully unmold onto a wire rack and let cool completely. Serve dusted with confectioners' sugar.

Store in an airtight container and eat within 3 days or freeze for up to 1 month. It can be lightly toasted under a broiler.

Variations:

Marbled Kugelhopf

Replace ⅓ cup of the white bread flour with ½ cup sifted unsweetened cocoa and 2 tablespoons sugar. Replace the 2½ oz. bittersweet chocolate with a similar quantity of white chocolate, coarsely chopped. Proceed as in the main recipe.

Golden Raisin Kugelhopf

Replace ⅓ cup of the white bread flour with ½ cup sifted unsweetened cocoa and 2 tablespoons sugar. Replace the 2½ oz. bittersweet chocolate with a similar quantity of golden raisins or raisins. Proceed as in the main recipe.

Note: *Both cocoa variations of this recipe are delicious toasted and spread with peanut butter.*

This pretty, yeast coffee-time cake is made in a traditional earthenware mold, a tube pan, or non-stick ring mold. Serve it either plain or toasted.

A *great* combination of ginger in syrup and bittersweet chocolate.
chocolate gingerbread

5½ oz. bittersweet chocolate

1⅓ sticks (¾ cup plus
1 tablespoon) sweet butter,
at room temperature

¾ cup sugar

3 large eggs, separated

½ cup plus 1 tablespoon
ground almonds

¾ cup plus 1½ tablespoons
self-rising flour

1 tablespoon unsweetened cocoa

3 pieces preserved ginger,
chopped, and 2 tablespoons
syrup from jar

Chocolate Topping:

1½ oz. bittersweet chocolate

1 tablespoon sweet butter

1 piece of preserved ginger,
sliced, and 1 tablespoon syrup
from the jar, to finish

one loaf pan, 8½ x 4½ x 3 inches,
greased and lined with
baking parchment

Chop the chocolate and melt very gently melt in a heatproof bowl set over a pan of steaming water. Stir until smooth, remove from the heat, and let cool. Using an electric mixer or wooden spoon, beat the butter until creamy, then gradually beat in the sugar. Beat until light and fluffy, then beat in the egg yolks one at a time, beating well after each addition.

Beat in the cooled chocolate, then sift the almonds, flour, and cocoa into the bowl. Add the chopped ginger and syrup, and fold in using a large metal spoon.

Whisk the egg whites until stiff peaks form, then fold into the mixture in 3 batches.

Spoon the mixture into the prepared pan and smooth the surface. Bake in a preheated oven at 375°F for about 40 minutes or until a skewer inserted into the center of the cake comes out clean. Leave for 5 minutes, then turn out onto a wire rack and let cool completely.

To make the topping, chop the chocolate and melt it with the butter and ginger syrup in a heatproof bowl set over a pan of steaming water. Stir until smooth, then spoon over the top of the cake. When almost set, decorate with finely sliced, diced, or grated preserved ginger.

Store in an airtight container and eat within 1 week—it improves in taste after several days. If undecorated, it can be frozen for up to 1 month.

marbled fudge cake

½ stick (¼ cup) sweet butter

3 oz. graham crackers, crushed

Chocolate Mixture:

3 tablespoons sweet butter

4 oz. bittersweet chocolate

2 large eggs

¾ cup sugar

½ cup all-purpose flour

a pinch of salt

½ teaspoon baking powder

2–3 drops real vanilla extract

2 oz. walnut pieces or pecans

Vanilla Mixture:

1¾ tablespoons sweet butter

½ teaspoon real vanilla extract

⅓ cup cream cheese

4½ tablespoons sugar

1 large egg, beaten

1 tablespoon all-purpose flour

one 8¼-inch springform pan, greased

Makes 1 cake (16 slices)

To make the base, melt the butter and mix with the cracker crumbs, then press into the base of the pan to make a thin, even layer. Chill while preparing the filling.

To make the chocolate mixture, dice the butter and bring to room temperature. Chop the chocolate and melt gently in a heatproof bowl set over a pan of barely simmering water. Stir until smooth, remove from the heat, and stir in the butter.

In another bowl beat the eggs and sugar with a wooden spoon until frothy. Sift the flour, salt, and baking powder into the bowl and stir well. Add the melted chocolate mixture and the vanilla. Chop the nuts, add to the bowl, and mix well. Spread over the base.

To make the vanilla mixture, bring the butter to room temperature, then beat until creamy using a wooden spoon or electric mixer. Beat in the vanilla and cream cheese until the mixture is light and fluffy. Gradually beat in the sugar, then the egg. Add the flour and stir well. Spoon on top of the chocolate and swirl the tip of a knife through the mixtures giving a marbled effect.

Bake in a preheated oven at 350°F for about 25 minutes until just firm. Let cool in the pan before unmolding. Serve at room temperature. Store in an airtight container and eat within 5 days, or freeze for up to 1 month.

This cake *improves* in flavor for several days after baking.

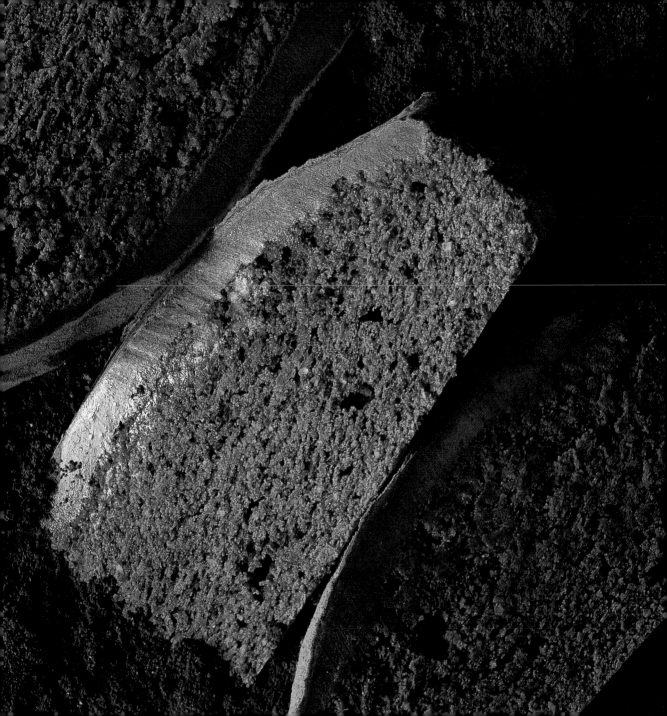

espresso cake

Sift the flour with the cocoa, salt, coffee, and ground almonds. In a mixing bowl, beat the butter until creamy using a wooden spoon or electric mixer. Gradually beat in the sugar. When light and fluffy, beat in the eggs, 1 tablespoon at a time. Carefully fold in the dry ingredients, hot water, and alcohol. Spoon into the prepared springform pan and smooth the surface. Bake in a preheated oven at 350°F for about 40 minutes, or until a skewer inserted into the center of the cake comes out clean. Carefully loosen the cake then unclip the pan. Let cool on a wire rack. To make the frosting, heat the cream until scalding hot, then remove from the heat and add the chocolate and coffee or alcohol. Leave until completely melted then stir gently. When cool and thick enough to spread, use to cover the top and sides of the cake. Leave until set, then store in an airtight container overnight before cutting. Eat within 1 week, or freeze for up to 1 month.

Finely **ground** *espresso coffee rather than liquid coffee may seem a rather odd ingredient for this* **moist** *cake—but it tastes extraordinarily good!*

1½ cups self-rising flour

1 cup minus 1 tablespoon unsweetened cocoa

a pinch of salt

1 tablespoon very finely ground espresso coffee

1⅓ cups ground almonds

2 sticks (1 cup) sweet butter

1 cup plus 2½ tablespoons superfine or granulated sugar

4 large eggs, beaten

3 tablespoons very hot water

1 tablespoon coffee liqueur or brandy (optional)

Chocolate Frosting:

⅔ cup heavy cream

5½ oz. bittersweet chocolate, chopped

1 tablespoon very strong black coffee, coffee liqueur, or brandy

one 9½-inch springform pan, greased and lined with baking parchment

Makes 1 cake

Make this soft, moist, *flourless cake* with macadamias, pecans, walnuts, almonds, or hazelnuts.
fudgy nut cake

12 oz. bittersweet chocolate

1½ sticks (¾ cup)
sweet butter, diced

½ cup unsweetened cocoa, sifted

3½ oz. mixture of nuts

5 large eggs

1 teaspoon real vanilla extract

1¼ cups sugar

confectioners' sugar and
unsweetened cocoa, for dusting

one 8½-inch springform pan,
greased and lined with
baking parchment

Makes 1 cake

Chop the chocolate and put into a heatproof bowl together with the diced butter. Set over a pan of steaming water and stir frequently until melted and smooth. Remove from the heat, stir in the cocoa, then let cool.

Meanwhile, coarsely chop the nuts. Put the eggs, vanilla, and sugar into a large heatproof bowl and beat briefly until frothy. Set the bowl over a pan of steaming water—the water should not touch the base of the bowl. Using an electric egg beater, beat the mixture until it is very pale and thick—when the beater is lifted it should leave a visible ribbon-like trail.

Remove the bowl from the heat, and beat for a couple of minutes so the mixture cools. Using a large metal spoon, carefully fold in the chocolate mixture, followed by the nuts. When thoroughly combined, spoon into the prepared springform pan and smooth the surface.

Bake in a preheated oven at 350°F for about 35 minutes or until firm to the touch but moist inside (do not overcook or the cake will be dry and hard to slice).

Let cool in the pan, then turn out and serve, dusted with cocoa and confectioners' sugar.

Store in an airtight container and eat within 1 week. It does not freeze well.

Rum-soaked golden raisins, butter, sugar, flour, and cocoa—a **terrific combination.** *Don't worry if the fruit sinks during baking.*

chocolate pound cake

3 oz. golden raisins

3 tablespoons rum

4 large eggs, at room temperature

about 2 sticks (1 cup) plus
2 tablespoons sweet butter,
at room temperature

about 1¼ cups superfine or
granulated sugar

½ cup unsweetened cocoa

about 1⅓ cups self-rising flour

a pinch of salt

one 2 lb. loaf pan, lined with
a double thickness of
greased wax paper

Makes 1 large cake

Soak the golden raisins in the rum, cover, and leave overnight. The next day, weigh the 4 eggs together and use exactly the same weight of butter and sugar.

Add to the cocoa enough of the flour to make the same weight. Sift the cocoa, flour, and salt twice.

Put the measured soft butter in the bowl of an electric mixer and beat until creamy. Gradually beat in the measured sugar. After the last addition beat the mixture until it becomes very white and light in texture.

Beat the eggs in a separate bowl, then beat into the butter mixture, 1 tablespoon at a time, beating well after each addition. Using a large metal spoon, fold in the sifted flour mixture very gently. When thoroughly combined, fold in the golden raisins and any rum left in the bowl.

Spoon into the prepared pan and smooth the surface. Bake in a preheated oven at 400°F for 40 to 50 minutes or until a cocktail stick or skewer comes out clean.

Cool the cake in the pan for a couple of minutes, then lift it out and peel off the paper. Let cool completely on a wire rack. Store in an airtight container and eat within 1 week, or freeze for up to 1 month.

devil's food cake

Chop the chocolate and gently melt with the butter, sugar, and syrup in a heavy pan over low heat, stirring frequently. Remove from the heat and let cool.

Sift the flour, cocoa, and baking soda into a mixing bowl and make a well in the center. Pour in the melted mixture, stir gently, then add the eggs, vanilla, and milk. Beat very gently with a wooden spoon until well mixed.

Spoon the mixture into the prepared pans and spread evenly. Bake in a preheated oven at 325°F for about 15 to 20 minutes until just firm to the touch. Let cool, then turn out of the pans.

To make the frosting, chop the chocolate. Heat the milk and sugar, stirring until dissolved, then boil rapidly for 1 minute until syrupy. Remove from the heat and stir in the chocolate. When melted and smooth, stir in the butter and vanilla. Let cool, stirring occasionally, then beat well until very thick.

Spread one-third of this mixture onto one of the cakes and set the second on top. Spread the rest of the mixture evenly over the top and sides. Leave in a cool spot (not the fridge) until set. Store in an airtight container and eat within 5 days.

The undecorated cakes can be frozen for up to 1 month.

An unusual, *quick*, and *easy* method that produces a very dark cake—yet *light* and full of flavor.

3 oz. bittersweet chocolate

1 stick (½ cup) sweet butter

7 tablespoons dark brown sugar

1 tablespoon golden syrup* or dark corn syrup

1 cup plus 2 tablespoons all-purpose flour

¼ cup unsweetened cocoa

½ teaspoon baking soda

2 large eggs, beaten

½ teaspoon real vanilla extract

½ cup minus 1 tablespoon milk

Chocolate Frosting:

2½ oz. bittersweet chocolate

⅔ cup whole milk

½ cup sugar

½ stick (¼ cup) sweet butter, at room temperature

½ teaspoon real vanilla extract

two 7-inch sandwich pans, greased and lined with baking parchment

Makes 1 cake

*Available in larger supermarkets.

chocolate crackles

4 oz. bittersweet chocolate,
coarsely chopped

1 stick (½ cup) sweet butter,
diced, at room temperature

1 large egg

2–3 drops real vanilla extract

¾ cup plus 2 tablespoons
light brown sugar

1 cup plus 2 tablespoons
self-rising flour

½ teaspoon baking soda

about 2 tablespoons
confectioners' sugar, for coating

several baking trays, greased

Makes about 28

Melt the chopped chocolate gently in a heatproof bowl set over a pan of barely simmering water, stirring frequently. Remove the bowl from the heat and gradually stir in the butter. In another bowl, beat the egg and vanilla until frothy using a wire whisk or electric mixer. Gradually beat in the sugar, followed by the chocolate mixture.

Sift the flour and baking soda into the bowl, then stir in to make a firm dough. In hot weather or if the dough seems sticky, wrap it and chill for 15 minutes.

Using your hands, roll the dough into walnut-sized balls. Roll each ball in confectioners' sugar, then arrange, spaced well apart, on the prepared baking trays.

Bake in a preheated oven at 400°F for about 10 to 12 minutes until just firm.

Cool for 1 minute until firm enough to transfer to a wire rack to cool completely.

Store in an airtight container and eat within 1 week, or freeze for up to 1 month.

These biscuits crack and spread in the oven—finish with a dusting of confectioners' sugar to make them look even more dramatic.

*Cut these shortbread cookies into any **pretty** shape,*
*then bake, cool, and **dip** in chocolate.*

cinnamon
chocolate stars

Using a wooden spoon or electric mixer beat the butter until creamy. Gradually beat in the sugar. When the mixture is pale and fluffy, sift the flour, salt, cinnamon, and rice flour into the bowl and mix. When the mixture comes together, turn it onto a lightly floured surface and knead lightly and briefly to make a smooth, but not sticky dough. In hot weather, or if the dough feels sticky, wrap it and chill until firm.
Roll out the dough to about ¼ inch thick and cut out shapes with the cutter. Gently knead together the trimmings, then re-roll and cut more stars.
Arrange the stars slightly apart on the prepared baking trays. Prick with a fork and chill for about 15 minutes.
Bake the cookies in a preheated oven at 350°F for about 12 to 15 minutes or until firm and barely colored.
Let cool on the baking trays for a couple of minutes until firm enough to transfer to a wire cooling rack.
When completely cold, gently melt the chocolate in a small heatproof bowl set over a pan of steaming water. Stir until smooth, then remove the bowl from the heat. Dip the points of the stars in to the melted chocolate, then leave to set on waxed paper, non-stick parchment, or a wire rack.
When firm, store in an airtight container and eat within 3 days. Undecorated cookies can be frozen for up to 1 month.

1½ sticks (¾ cup) plus
1 tablespoon sweet butter,
at room temperature

7 tablespoons sugar

1½ cups all-purpose flour

a good pinch of salt

1 teaspoon ground cinnamon

5 tablespoons rice flour
or cornstarch

2 oz. bittersweet chocolate,
to finish

one star-shaped cookie cutter

several baking trays, greased

Makes 30

black and white
cookies

1 stick (½ cup) sweet butter, at room temperature

7 tablespoons light brown sugar

1 large egg, beaten

6½ tablespoons self-rising flour

½ teaspoon baking powder

a pinch of salt

½ teaspoon real vanilla extract

1½ cups rolled oats

6½ oz. bittersweet chocolate, chopped into chunks

several baking trays, greased

Makes about 24

Beat the butter until creamy using a wooden spoon or electric mixer. Add the sugar and beat until light and creamy. Gradually beat in the egg, and beat well after the last addition. Sift the flour with the baking powder and salt into the mixing bowl, add the vanilla extract and oats, and stir in. When thoroughly combined, stir in the chocolate chunks. Put heaped teaspoons of the mixture, spaced well apart, onto the prepared trays, then bake in a preheated oven at 350°F for 12 to 15 minutes until golden and just firm.

Let cool on the trays for a couple of minutes until firm enough to transfer to a wire rack.

Let cool completely, then store in an airtight container. Eat within 1 week or freeze for up to 1 month.

*Make chocolate chips by chopping good **bittersweet** chocolate into large chunks—the flavor is far **superior** to the commercial chocolate chips.*

*Chocolate chip cookies with a difference—the dough is flavored with **melted** bittersweet chocolate plus chocolate **chunks.***

giant double chocolate
nut cookies

5 oz. bittersweet chocolate, chopped

7 tablespoons sweet butter, at room temperature

6½ tablespoons superfine or granulated sugar

6½ tablespoons dark brown sugar

1 large egg, beaten

½ teaspoon real vanilla extract

1 cup all-purpose flour

a pinch of salt

½ teaspoon baking powder

2 oz. pecans or walnuts, chopped

3½ oz. unsweetened (or white) chocolate, chopped into chunks

several baking trays, greased

Makes 16

In a heatproof bowl, gently melt the 5 oz. chopped chocolate over a pan of barely simmering water. Remove from the heat and let cool.

Meanwhile beat the butter until creamy using a wooden spoon or electric mixer. Add the sugars and beat again until light and fluffy. Gradually beat in the egg and vanilla extract, followed by the melted chocolate.

Sift the flour into the bowl with the salt and baking powder and stir. When thoroughly combined, work in the chopped nuts and chocolate chunks.

Put heaped tablespoons of dough, spaced well apart, onto the prepared baking trays.

Bake in a preheated oven at 350°F for about 12 to 15 minutes until just firm. Cool for a couple of minutes until firm enough to transfer to a wire rack to cool completely.

Store in an airtight container. Eat within 1 week or freeze for up to 1 month.

squillionaire's
shortbread

14 oz. canned condensed milk

1 stick (½ cup) sweet butter,
at room temperature

5 tablespoons sugar

1 cup plus 1 tablespoon
all-purpose flour

3 tablespoons unsweetened cocoa

Chocolate Topping:

6 oz. bittersweet chocolate

2 tablespoons sweet butter, diced

about 2 oz. white chocolate,
to finish

one square, 9-inch cake pan,
2 inches deep, greased

Makes 16

To make the filling, put the unopened can of condensed milk in a heavy pan and cover with water. Bring to a boil, then simmer without covering the pan for 3½ hours. Top up the water regularly: the can must always be covered. Cool the can completely before opening. The condensed milk should have become a fudgy, dark, golden caramel.

Meanwhile, to make the chocolate cookie base, beat the butter until creamy, then beat in the sugar. When the mixture is light and fluffy, sift the flour with the cocoa into the bowl and work with your hands to make a smooth dough. Press the dough into the prepared cake pan to make an even layer. Prick well with a fork and chill for 15 minutes.

Bake the cookie base in a preheated oven at 350°F for 20 minutes until just firm and slightly darker around the edges—do not overcook or it will taste bitter.

Let cool in the pan. When completely cold, spread the cold caramel over the top. Chill until firm—about 1 to 2 hours.

To make the topping, chop the chocolate and melt in a heatproof bowl set over a pan of barely simmering water. Remove from the heat and stir in the butter. When smooth, spread over the caramel, then leave to set. Melt the white chocolate in the same way, then drizzle over the top of the dark chocolate using a fork or a wax paper frosting bag. Leave overnight until firm, then cut. Store in an airtight container and eat within 1 week. Not suitable for freezing.

three-chocolate
squares

Chop the chocolate and melt gently in a heatproof bowl set over a pan of barely simmering water. Stir occasionally. Remove the bowl from the heat and let cool.

Meanwhile beat the butter until creamy with a wooden spoon or electric mixer. Add the sugar and vanilla and beat well. Gradually beat in the egg, followed by the cooled chocolate.

Sift the flour with the baking powder, baking soda, and cocoa into another bowl.

Using a metal spoon, fold the flour mixture into the chocolate mixture in 3 batches alternating with the sour cream.

When thoroughly combined, spoon into the prepared pan and smooth the surface.

Bake in a preheated oven at 375°F until just firm—about 25 to 30 minutes. Let cool in the pan before turning out.

To make the topping, melt the white chocolate as before, then stir in the butter. When smooth, spread over the cake and leave until set.

Cut into 16 pieces and store in an airtight container. Eat within 5 days or freeze for up to 1 month.

Three *kinds of chocolate—white,*
bittersweet, and cocoa—make
great **treats**, *good with coffee.*

2½ oz. bittersweet chocolate

1 stick (½ cup),
at room temperature

¾ cup plus 1 tablespoon light brown sugar

½ teaspoon real vanilla extract

1 large egg, beaten

1½ cups all-purpose flour

1 teaspoon baking powder

½ teaspoon baking soda

¼ cup unsweetened cocoa

⅔ cup sour cream

White Chocolate Topping:

2 oz. good quality white chocolate, chopped

1½ tablespoons sweet butter,
at room temperature

one square, 8-inch cake pan,
greased and lined with
baking parchment

Makes 16

fudge brownies

1¼ sticks (½ cup plus
2 tablespoons) sweet butter

4 large eggs, beaten

1¾ cups light brown sugar

1 teaspoon real vanilla extract

a good pinch of salt

¾ cup unsweetened cocoa

1 cup minus 1 tablespoon
all-purpose flour

3½ oz. walnut or pecan pieces,
chopped white or bittersweet
chocolate, or a combination

one square, 9-inch cake pan,
2 inches deep, completely lined
with foil

Makes 16

Gently melt the butter in a pan and let cool while preparing the rest of the mixture.

Using a wooden spoon, beat the eggs very gently with the sugar until just blended and free of lumps. Stir in the cooled butter and the vanilla. Sift the salt, cocoa, and flour together into the bowl and gently stir in—do not beat or overmix, or the brownies will become cake-like.

When combined, fold in the nuts or chocolate. Pour into the prepared pan and smooth the surface.

Bake in a preheated oven at 325°F for about 35 to 40 minutes or until a skewer inserted midway between the center and the side of the pan comes out clean. The center should be just firm—do not overcook or the brownies will be dry.

Put the pan on a damp cloth to cool completely.

Lift the brownies out of the pan still in the foil, remove the foil, and cut into 16 squares.

Store in an airtight container and eat within 1 week or freeze for up to 1 month.

A wonderful version of one of the great **American** classics.

blondies

1¼ sticks (½ cup plus 2 tablespoons) sweet butter

2 cups light brown sugar

1 teaspoon real vanilla extract

3 large eggs, beaten

2 cups all-purpose flour

1 teaspoon baking powder

a large pinch of salt

2 oz. walnut pieces, coarsely chopped

2 oz. good white chocolate, coarsely chopped

2 oz. bittersweet chocolate, coarsely chopped

one 12 x 8½ inch roasting or baking pan, lined with foil

Makes 48

Put the butter into a large, heavy saucepan and melt gently. Add the sugar, stir well, then remove from the heat. Cool for 1 minute, then stir in the vanilla extract and the eggs.

Sift the flour, baking powder, and salt into the saucepan and stir just until thoroughly blended—do not beat or overmix.

Pour the mixture into the prepared baking pan and spread evenly. Sprinkle the nuts and chopped chocolate over the top.

Bake in a preheated oven at 350°F for about 25 minutes until just firm.

Cool for a few minutes in the pan then lift the cake, still in the foil, onto a wire rack to cool completely.

Remove the foil and cut into 48 squares. Store in an airtight container and eat within 4 days. They can be frozen for up to 1 month, but they will be stickier than freshly baked ones.

Pale-gold *brownies, topped with nuts and two kinds of chocolate—**dark** and **white**.*

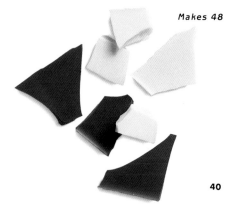

A delicate mixture flavored with finely ground coffee.
mocha madeleines

Chop the chocolate and melt gently with the butter in a heatproof bowl set over a pan of barely simmering water, stirring frequently. Remove from the heat and let cool. Meanwhile, sift the flour twice with the cocoa, salt, and coffee, then set aside. Using an electric mixer, beat the eggs with the sugar until the mixture becomes pale and thick—when the beater is lifted out, the mixture should leave a ribbon-like trail on the surface.

Using a large metal spoon, fold the flour mixture into the egg mixture in 3 batches, then carefully fold in the chocolate mixture until all are thoroughly combined (the mixture will lose a little bulk).

Put a heaped teaspoon or so of the mixture into each madeleine mold so it is two-thirds full.

Bake in a preheated oven at 375°F for about 10 to 12 minutes or until just firm. Let cool for 1 minute, then remove from the molds using a table knife.

Cool on a wire rack, then dust with confectioners' sugar. Store in an airtight container and eat within 1 week or freeze for up to 1 month.

Note: *Non-stick madeleine molds work best. If using ordinary metal molds, brush them with 2 coats of melted butter and chill between applications.*

3 oz. bittersweet chocolate

1¼ sticks (½ cup plus 2 tablespoons) sweet butter, diced

1 cup minus 1 tablespoon all-purpose flour

2 tablespoons unsweetened cocoa

a pinch of salt

1 teaspoon finely ground espresso coffee

4 large eggs

¾ cup minus 1 tablespoon sugar

confectioners' sugar, for dusting

madeleine molds, twice-buttered

Makes 30

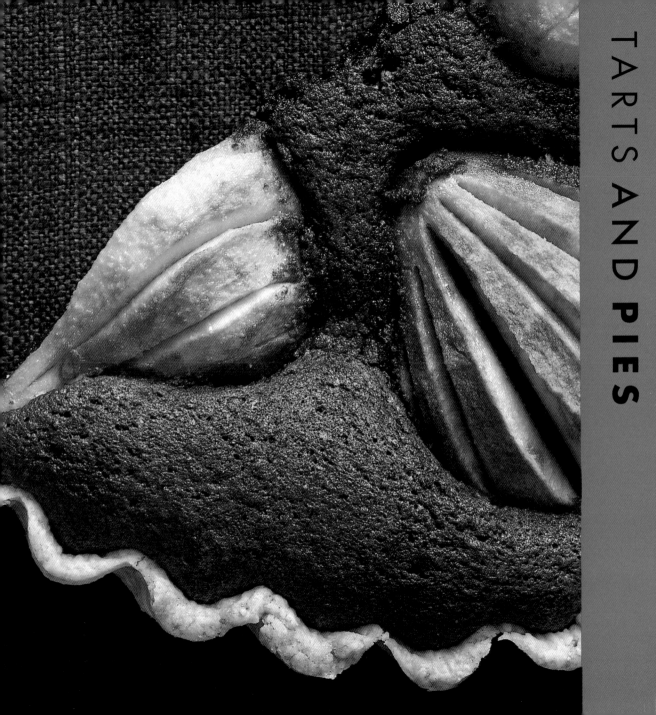

chocolate pear tart

1 cup plus 3 tablespoons
all-purpose flour

1 stick (½ cup) sweet butter,
chilled and diced

2½ tablespoons sugar

1 egg yolk

about 1 tablespoon ice water

Chocolate Pear Filling:

4½ oz. bittersweet chocolate,
chopped

1 stick (½ cup), plus 1 tablespoon
sweet butter, at room temperature

7 tablespoons sugar

4 large eggs, separated

1¼ cups plus 2 tablespoons
ground almonds

2–3 drops real almond extract

a pinch of salt

2 ripe medium-sized pears

one deep, 9-inch
false-bottom tart pan

one baking tray

Makes 1 tart, serves 8

To make the pastry, sift the flour into a bowl, and rub in the diced butter with the tips of your fingers until the mixture resembles fine crumbs.

Stir in the sugar, add the egg yolk and water, then bind the mixture together using a table knife or pastry blender. If the dough is dry and crumbly, add a little extra water.

Without kneading, quickly bring the dough together with your hands to make a soft but not sticky ball.

To make the dough in a food processor, put the flour, butter, and sugar into the bowl and process until the mixture resembles fine crumbs. With the machine running, add the yolk and water through the feed tube and process just until the dough comes together.

Wrap and chill the dough for 20 minutes. On a lightly floured surface, roll out the pastry to a circle 11½ inches across. Line the tart pan with it. Chill while preparing the filling.

Put a baking tray into a preheated oven 400°F to heat up— this helps to make the tart shell crisp.

To make the filling, very gently melt the chocolate in a heatproof bowl set over a pan of barely simmering water. Stir until smooth, then remove from the heat and let cool.

Meanwhile, using an electric mixer or wooden spoon, beat the butter until creamy, then beat in the sugar. When the mixture is light and fluffy, beat in the egg yolks one at a time, beating well after each addition. Beat in the cooled chocolate, then stir in the almonds and extract using a large metal spoon.

In a very clean greasefree bowl, beat the egg whites with the pinch of salt until they form soft peaks. Using a large metal spoon, gently fold them into the chocolate mixture in 3 batches. Spoon into the prepared chilled tart shell and spread evenly.

Peel and halve the pears, then scoop out the cores with a melon-baller or pointed teaspoon. Thinly slice the pear halves, leaving the slices attached at the stalk end, so they resemble fans. Arrange the pears on top of the chocolate mixture in a neat pattern.

Set the tart pan on the heated baking tray and bake for 15 minutes, then reduce the oven temperature to 350°F and bake for about 10 minutes longer or until just cooked in the center—test with a skewer.

Very carefully unmold and serve either warm or at room temperature with crème fraîche or vanilla ice-cream. The tart tastes better the day after baking, though it sinks slightly.

Variation:

Chocolate Normandy Tart

Substitute crisp, tart apples for the pears and prepare them in the same way. Add ½ teaspoon ground cinnamon to the chocolate filling, and proceed as in the main recipe.

Use just-ripe Comice pears for this rich, not-too-sweet tart.

Serve warm, at room temperature, or **chilled** *with vanilla ice cream, crème fraîche, or chocolate sauce.*

chestnut and chocolate
moneybags

about 10½ oz. filo pastry

7 oz. bittersweet chocolate

1 cup plus 1 tablespoon
curd cheese, such as ricotta

3 tablespoons dark brown sugar

2 egg yolks

2–3 tablespoons rum

4 oz. drained cooked chestnuts,
roughly chopped (vacuum-packed
or canned in light syrup or water)

½ stick (¼ cup sweet butter,
melted, for brushing

confectioners' sugar for dusting

several baking trays

Makes 12, serves 4–6

If necessary defrost the pastry according to the package instructions. (Filo varies enormously between brands—some are very good: others turn out tough and leathery. Ask advice from other cooks about the best local brands.)

To make the filling, grate the chocolate coarsely and set aside. Beat the curd cheese until softened using a wooden spoon, then beat in the sugar followed by the egg yolks. Add rum to taste. Using a metal spoon, gently stir in the grated chocolate and the chestnuts.

Remove the pastry from the box and cover with a damp cloth until ready to use—the sheets of dough dry out very easily and become unusable. Put 3 sheets on a work surface and cut into 7-inch squares. Put a heaped tablespoon of the mixture (¹⁄₁₂ of the amount) into the center of each square, gather up the edges, and twist the top to resemble a pastry money bag. There is no need to dampen the edges of the pastry. Repeat to make 12. Arrange, spaced well apart on the baking trays and chill for about 15 minutes.

Brush with melted butter, then bake in a preheated oven at 375°F for about 15 minutes until golden brown. Serve, dusted with confectioners' sugar.

southern deep-dish
pecan pie

1 cup plus 3 tablespoons
all-purpose flour

a pinch of salt

1 stick (½ cup) sweet butter,
chilled and diced

2½ tablespoons sugar

1 egg yolk

1 tablespoon ice water, to bind

Pecan Filling:

1 cup plus 1½ tablespoons
light brown sugar

1¼ cups heavy cream

2½ oz. bittersweet chocolate,
chopped

2 egg yolks

½ teaspoon real vanilla extract

1 tablespoon bourbon (optional)

1½ cups pecan halves

shaved or grated white chocolate
"curls", to finish

one false-bottom, deep,
9-inch tart pan

Makes 1 pie, serves 8–10

If using a food processor, put the flour and salt into the bowl.
Add the butter and process until fine crumbs are formed. Add
the sugar and process briefly. With the machine running, add
the egg yolk and water and process until the dough comes
together. Wrap and chill for 20 minutes until firm.

Roll out the dough to a large circle about 11½ inches across
and use to line the tart pan. Prick well and chill for about
15 minutes.

To bake the pastry blind, fill with a round of parchment paper
and baking beans and cook in a preheated oven at 400°F for
about 15 minutes until firm. Remove the paper and beans and
return the pie shell, still in its pan, to the oven for about
5–10 minutes until crisp and golden. Let cool.

To prepare the filling, put the sugar and cream into a heavy
pan and stir over medium heat until the sugar has melted and
the mixture is almost boiling. Remove from the heat and stir
in the chocolate. When smooth add the egg yolks and mix
well. Stir over very low heat until the mixture thickens.
Remove from the heat and stir in the vanilla, bourbon (if
using), and nuts. Pour into the prepared pie shell and chill
until firm. Serve decorated with white chocolate curls (these
are made using a vegetable peeler or grater).

A pecan pie with **nuts**, *chocolate,* and ***bourbon.***

amaretti chocolate
cheesecake pie

To make the crust, mix the butter and crushed amaretti crumbs then press onto the base of the prepared pan in an even layer. Chill while making the filling.

To make the filling, chop the chocolate and melt it gently in a heatproof bowl set over a pan of steaming water. Remove from the heat, stir until smooth, then let cool.

Put the cream cheese, eggs, and sugar into the bowl of a food processor and process until thoroughly combined. Add the cream and process again until just mixed. With the machine running add the melted chocolate and amaretto, if using, through the feed tube, and process until smooth.

Spoon the filling into the prepared pan and smooth the surface. Bake in a preheated oven at 325°F for 40 minutes until firm. Let cool in the oven with the door ajar. When completely cold, chill overnight.

Unclip the pan and remove the cheesecake. Decorate the top with the broken amaretti cookies. Drizzle with the melted chocolate, using either a wax paper frosting bag with the end snipped off, or a fork dipped in the chocolate.

Store the cheesecake in a covered container in the fridge then remove 30 minutes before serving. Eat within 5 days or freeze for up to 1 month.

Amaretti add crunchy texture and nutty taste to this easy recipe.

½ stick (¼ cup) sweet butter, melted

3½ oz. amaretti cookies, crushed, plus 6 extra, broken, to finish

1½ oz. bittersweet chocolate, melted, to drizzle

Chocolate Filling:

7 oz. bittersweet chocolate

1¾ cups cream cheese

2 eggs

5 tablespoons sugar

⅞ cup heavy cream

¼ cup amaretto liqueur (optional)

one 8½-inch springform pan, greased

Serves 12

A thoroughly **self-indulgent,** *grown-up version of a traditional English nursery pudding.*

chocolate
rice pudding

1 oz. bittersweet chocolate, chopped

2½ cups whole milk

2½ tablespoons short-grained rice

2 tablespoons superfine or granulated sugar

1 vanilla bean*

one 3-cup ovenproof baking dish, very well buttered

Serves 4

The vanilla bean can be rinsed carefully, dried, then used again.

Heat the chocolate and milk gently in a pan just until melted, stirring occasionally. Let cool. Put the rice, sugar, and vanilla bean in the buttered dish and pour in the chocolate milk. Stir gently, then bake in a preheated oven at 300°F for about 2½ hours until the rice is tender and the pudding thickened. Serve warm.

Variation:

Chocolate Rice Cream

This variation is cooked on top of the stove. Omit the vanilla bean and put the remaining ingredients in a saucepan with 3 green cardamom pods. Bring to a boil, stirring, then simmer for 40 minutes until the rice is soft. Remove the cardamom. Stir in 1 egg yolk and cook 1 minute. Pour into a large serving dish or small dishes, cool, cover, and chill. Serve ice cold, sprinkled with confectioners' sugar or a drizzle of cream.

hot white
chocolate pudding

Melt the chopped chocolate in a heatproof bowl set over a pan of barely simmering water. Remove from the heat and stir until smooth.

Using a wooden spoon or electric mixer, beat the butter until creamy, then gradually beat in the sugar. When the mixture is very light and fluffy, beat in the eggs, 1 tablespoon at a time, beating well after each addition.

Using a metal spoon, carefully fold in the flour and salt, then fold in the melted chocolate, vanilla extract, and enough milk to give a soft, dropping consistency.

Spoon into the prepared dish—it should be two-thirds full. Cover loosely with buttered foil and bake in a preheated oven at 350°F for about 35 minutes or until firm.

Meanwhile, to make the chocolate custard, heat the milk in a saucepan until scalding hot. Sift the cocoa, sugar, and cornstarch into a bowl and mix to a thick paste with the egg yolks and about 1 tablespoon of the milk.

Stir in the remaining milk, then return the mixture to the pan. Stir over low heat until very hot, thickened, and smooth—do not allow to boil. Serve immediately with the pudding.

A cold weather *treat*—baked chocolate sponge pudding, served with chocolate *custard*.

3 oz. white chocolate, chopped

1 stick (½ cup) sweet butter, at room temperature

½ cup plus 1 tablespoon superfine or granulated sugar

2 large eggs, beaten

1 cup self-rising flour

a pinch of salt

a few drops real vanilla extract

about 3 tablespoons milk

Chocolate Custard:

1¾ cups whole milk

3 tablespoons unsweetened cocoa

4 tablespoons superfine or granulated sugar

2 tablespoons cornstarch

2 egg yolks

one 3-cup baking dish, well greased

Serves 4

A wonderfully rich, light, smooth soufflé with a surprise filling.
rich chocolate soufflé

Brush melted butter inside the ramekins and sprinkle with superfine sugar. Stand on a baking tray or in a roasting pan. Put the chocolate and cream into a heavy-based pan. Set over very low heat and stir occasionally until melted. Remove from the heat and stir gently until smooth. Gently stir in the egg yolks, one at a time, then half the brandy or liqueur.

Put the 5 egg whites into a very clean, grease-free bowl and beat until stiff peaks form. Sprinkle with the sugar and briefly beat again to make a smooth, stiff meringue. If you over-beat the meringue at this stage it will do more harm than good, and the end result will be less smooth.

The chocolate mixture should be just warm, so gently reheat it if necessary. Using a large metal spoon, mix in a little of the meringue to loosen the consistency. Pour the chocolate mixture on top of the meringue and gently fold together until thoroughly combined but not over-mixed.

Half-fill the prepared ramekins. Spoon the remaining brandy or liqueur over the amaretti cookies then put one in the center of each ramekin. Add the remaining mixture until the ramekins are full almost to the rim.

Bake in a preheated oven at 425°F for 8–10 minutes. Remove from the oven when they are barely set (the centers should be soft and wobble when gently shaken). Sprinkle with confectioners' sugar and serve immediately.

6 oz. bittersweet chocolate, broken into small squares

½ cup plus 1 tablespoon heavy cream

3 eggs, separated, plus 2 egg whites

4 tablespoons brandy or amaretto liqueur

3 tablespoons superfine or granulated sugar

4 amaretti cookies

confectioners' sugar, for sprinkling

four 1¼-cup ovenproof ramekin dishes, buttered and sugared (see method)

Serves 4

A velvety **smooth** *finale for a* **special** *dinner party—serve this terrine with very strong coffee.*

chocolate terrine

14 oz. bittersweet chocolate, coarsely chopped

½ cup plus 2 tablespoons unsweetened cocoa

3 tablespoons strong espresso coffee

2 tablespoons brandy

6 large eggs, at room temperature

½ cup sugar

1 cup heavy cream, chilled

one loaf pan, 8½ x 4½ x 3 inches deep, greased and lined with baking parchment

one bain-marie or roasting pan

Serves 8

Put the chopped chocolate into a heatproof bowl with the cocoa and coffee. Set over a pan of barely simmering water and melt gently, stirring frequently. Remove the bowl from the heat, stir in the brandy, and let cool.

Meanwhile put the eggs into the bowl of an electric mixer and beat until frothy. Add the sugar and beat until the mixture is pale and very thick—the beaters should leave a ribbon-like trail when lifted.

In another bowl, whip the cream until it holds a soft peak. Using a large metal spoon, gently fold the chocolate mixture into the eggs. When combined, fold in the whipped cream. Spoon the mixture into the prepared pan, then stand the pan in a bain-marie (a roasting pan half-filled with warm water). Bake in a preheated oven at 325°F for about 1 to 1¼ hours or until a skewer inserted into the center of the mixture comes out clean.

Remove from the oven, let cool in the bain-marie for about 45 minutes, then lift the pan out of the bain-marie and leave until completely cold.

Chill overnight then turn out. Serve dusted with confectioners' sugar. Store, well wrapped in the refrigerator, for up to 5 days.

This dessert is very rich*, so serve in* small *portions.*

chocolate brûlée

2¾ cups thick light cream or thin pouring heavy cream

1 vanilla bean, split

10½ oz. bittersweet chocolate, finely chopped

4 egg yolks

½ cup plus 1 tablespoon confectioners' sugar, sifted

about 3 tablespoons superfine or granulated sugar, for sprinkling

eight ⅔-cup ramekins

one bain-marie or roasting pan

Serves 8

In a heavy saucepan, heat the cream with the split vanilla bean until scalding hot but not boiling. Remove from the heat, cover, and leave to infuse for 15 minutes.

Lift out the vanilla bean and scrape the seeds into the cream with the tip of a small knife.

Stir the chocolate into the cream until melted and smooth.

Put the egg yolks and confectioners' sugar into a medium-sized bowl, beat with a wooden spoon until well blended, then stir in the warm chocolate cream. When thoroughly combined, pour into the ramekin dishes.

Stand the dishes in a bain-marie (a roasting pan half-filled with warm water) and bake in a preheated oven at 350°F for about 30 minutes until just firm. Remove from the bain-marie and let cool. Cover and chill overnight or for up to 48 hours.

Sprinkle a little sugar over the tops, then put under a very hot broiler for just a few minutes to caramelize. A warning: if the ramekins are left for too long under the broiler the chocolate cream will melt. Serve within 1 hour.